THE CREATIVE BOOK OF

Pressed Flowers

THE CREATIVE BOOK OF

Pressed Flowers

Mary Lawrence

a Salamander book

Published by Salamander Books Limited
LONDON • NEW YORK

Published by Salamander Books Limited,
129-137 York Way, London N7 9LG, United Kingdom

©Salamander Books Ltd. 1988
The copyright on floral designs belongs
exclusively to Mary Lawrence

ISBN 0 86101 389 1

CREDITS

Editor-in-chief: Jilly Glassborow

Editor: Coral Walker

Designer: Kathy Gummer

Photographer: Steve Tanner

Typeset by: The Old Mill, London

Colour separation by: Fotographics Ltd, London – Hong Kong

Printed in Belgium by: Proost International Book Production

CONTENTS

INTRODUCTION

Making pressed flower arrangements is such a delightful hobby
because it involves so much more than simply creating the
designs — much of the pleasure comes from the hours spent in
the garden cultivating the plants, the long lazy walks in the country
gathering wild flowers, and the preparation and pressing of the flowers
and foliage at home. And when it comes to making the designs
themselves, there is the pleasure of planning them — deciding which
flowers to use, what shapes to make, what colour schemes to create.

This colourful book will see you through all the various stages from
gathering the flowers to the finished design. There is information on
growing and gathering plants, which flowers are most suitable for
pressing, and how to make a press, press the flowers, create a greeting
card or mount and frame a design. There is also plenty of advice on the
various techniques you will need to employ when creating your designs.
And finally, there are the designs themselves — over 80 beautiful creations
from which to choose, ranging from easy-to-make Christmas and birthday
cards, through more complex pictures to some delightful novelty ideas
that make use of all kinds of items around the home.

In most cases plants have been given their common names, except in
those instances where the Latin name is more often used. But, as common
names can vary so much, the scientific names of plants have also been
given at the back of the book.

PRESSED FLOWERS

The way nature has fashioned flowers gives us great but short-lived pleasure and delight; capture this delight by pressing flowers and you will have the perfect medium for creating pictures of lasting beauty. To enjoy collecting and pressing you do not have to act like a botanist seeking specimens, but your enjoyment of the countryside will increase as you start to look more closely at what is growing there. Examine the structure of each flower you find and learn to appreciate, for instance, the beauty in a single floret of cow parsley or the exquisite detail in the veining of a rose leaf. Try also to learn the plants' names. You will soon discover which plants are most suitable for pressing and when best to pick them, and to help you, we have illustrated many of the most suitable and colourful ones on pages 22-23.

GATHERING WILD FLOWERS

There is an amazing variety of wild flowers, many of which you may have never previously noticed, and if you gather sparingly from the countryside, you will not harm the plant's future growth. However, do pay attention to the official list of protected plants that you may not pick. Don't break off stems or pull up roots, but cleanly cut the parts you require with scissors. If you place the cut flowers in an opaque plastic carrier bag, blow it up like a balloon and seal it, they will keep well for a few hours. Don't forget also to gather leaves, tendrils, stems, grasses and seedheads. Among the best leaves are those of carrot, meadowsweet, cow parsley, rose, wild strawberry, silverweed, vetch, cherry, maple, sumach and virginia creeper.

FLOWERS TO GROW OR BUY

Annuals, perennials, shrubs and trees all provide material for pressing and even if you only have a window box, you can sow alyssum, candytuft, forget-me-not, lobelia and polyanthus. Succulent and fleshy flowers contain too much moisture to press successfully. Multi-petalled or thick centred flowers such as roses, carnations, chrysanthemums and marguerites do not press satisfactorily as whole flowers but need to be broken into separate parts for pressing.

When picking flowers from the garden, lay them gently in a basket as you cut them, and then dry and press them as soon as possible.

You can still find flowers to press on wet days and in the winter months by visiting a florist where you can purchase a wide range of cut flowers, foliage and pot plants.

Even a small courtyard garden can yield a wide range of annuals, perennials, shrubs and trees to provide flowers and foliage to press.

——WHEN TO PICK AND PRESS——

The optimum time to pick flowers is at midday when all the dew has evaporated. Sunny weather is best and rainy days should be avoided. If you have to pick flowers in damp weather, pick whole stems, and stand them indoors in water for a few hours until the flowerheads are dry. Pick flowers at their best, when they have just opened (and before they produce pollen), and gather some buds as well. Look out for varying sizes, unusual shapes, a variety of tints and veining, and interesting visual textures. Remember as you are pressing that you can thin out collective flowerheads such as spiraea, candytuft, wild parsley and hydrangea, so do not pass over large headed flowers.

Bought flowers also need immediate attention, so don't be tempted to enjoy their beauty for a few days before pressing, but press them while they are at their best.

EQUIPMENT AND TECHNIQUES

Pressed flower arranging need not be an expensive hobby: the design elements (i.e. the flowers) can cost nothing and the equipment is relatively cheap; you can even make your own press at no great expense (see page 16). The amount of money you spend on a design depends largely on the cost of your setting.

Glassine photographic negative bags are ideal for storing your flowers as they are made from acid-free paper which will not attack the plant material. Aids for handling the flowers include a palette knife, tweezers and a paint brush. Miniature flowers like alyssum can be picked up with a needle point and moved about with a fine paint brush. Larger flowers can be picked up with a palette knife or a slightly dampened finger tip and then transferred to the grip of round-nosed tweezers. To fix flowers in a design use latex adhesive. Squeeze a small amount of adhesive on to a palette dish and use a cocktail stick or toothpick to transfer a small dot of

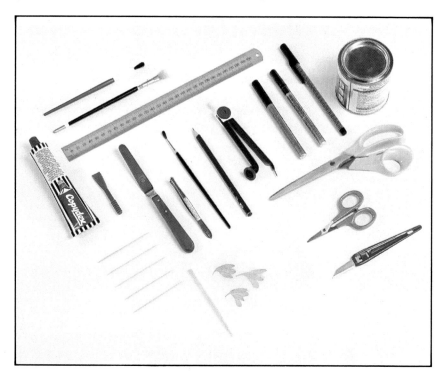

Equipment required for making pressed flower designs includes: latex adhesive and cocktail sticks; round-nosed tweezers and palette knife; large and small fine scissors; craft knife; ruler, pencil and compass; gold, silver and coloured marker pens; assorted paint brushes; varnish and, of course, flowers.

it on to the centre back of a flower. Now press the flower in position.

Sprays and larger flowers may need several dots of adhesive to hold them in place, although great care must be taken to ensure that no adhesive can be seen from the front of the flower. Discard and renew the latex as soon as it starts to set in the dish.

THE DESIGN BASE

All pictures must be formed on some base; this can be paper, fabric, wood, metal or plastic, and in this book it is referred to as the design base. In choosing textiles, remember that some man-made fabrics are unsuitable in both texture and colour. Old satins and silks are excellent, as are the range of velvets and fine cottons.

Art shops carry a great range of papers and boards. As a design base for pictures, parchment, marbled and watercolour papers are highly suitable. Rough textured watercolour papers and the many shades of heavyweight Ingres paper and twin-wire self-coloured boards are equally suitable for making greeting cards. To make a card, first cut a rectangle of paper or board to the required size, then score (make a crease) along the fold line. Lay your card face down on a cutting board and use a blunt instrument, such as a knitting needle or the blunt edge of a scissor blade to 'rule' firmly down the edge of a ruler, so making a crease in the paper. You can now easily fold along this line; if necessary trim the card after it has been folded. Before drawing on the card with a coloured pen it is advisable to mark out your border first in pencil.

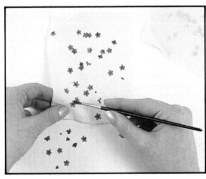

Large flowers can be picked up on the end of a slightly moistened finger tip before being gripped and moved about with round-nosed tweezers.

After pressing, small flowers can be removed from the tissue by bending the paper round a finger and lifting the flowers off with a paint brush.

To make you own press, cut two pieces of 10mm ($^3/_8$in) plywood measuring 275mm (10$^3/_4$in) square. Clamp them together and drill 5mm ($^3/_{16}$in) holes in each corner, 18mm ($^3/_4$in) from the sides. Open up the holes in the top square to 8mm ($^5/_{16}$in). Sand all surfaces, rounding the corners, and apply two coats of matt varnish.

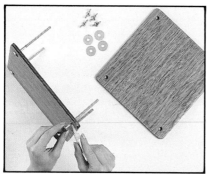

Purchase some 7mm by 200mm ($^1/_4$in by 8in) fully threaded bolts, with washers and wing-nuts (if not available you can use shorter bolts, 150mm (6in) long). The holes drilled in the bottom square are slightly undersize, but the bolts can be screwed in; add a little 'super' strong glue to the bottom threads just before screwing the bolts home, to fix them permanently.

Take some old newspapers and some thin, double-walled corrugated cardboard and cut them into rectangles 225mm by 255mm (9in by 10in). Cut sheets of blotting paper to the same size then assemble the press by sandwiching layers of blotting paper and newspaper between the cardboard. Each cardboard 'sandwich' should contain 12 sheets of newspaper with two sheets of blotting paper in the centre.

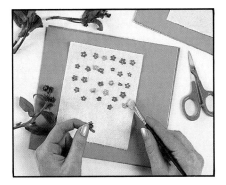

Small flowers and leaves should be placed face down on smooth toilet tissue on top of the blotting paper. Cover them with more tissue before covering with another sheet of blotting paper. Pick sprays of small flowers and press a few whole, but snip off the individual heads of the majority and arrange in rows on the toilet tissue as shown, using a paint brush to move them into position.

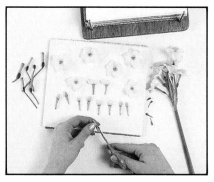

Larger flowers such as narcissus 'Sol d'Or' can be placed directly on to the blotting paper, having cut away all the harder parts with sharp scissors. Flowers pressed in profile need to be cut in half lengthways. Put a tab sticking out from between the layers in the press to identify what flowers you have in that layer or layers, and the date when they were put in.

Multi-petalled flowers such as roses and carnations must be broken down into separate petals before pressing and, depending on their size, should be pressed directly between either blotting paper or toilet tissue. The stems, sepals and bracts should be pressed separately in a press devoted to thick items. Use twice as much newspaper as usual between the layers in this press.

Not all leaves are suitable for pressing (see page 12), and of those that are, usually only the younger ones are used. An exception is autumn coloured leaves which often have part of their water content already removed naturally, due to the season. As with flowers, cut or pull the leaves from the stems and arrange neatly on the paper. If they are thick, put them in a press reserved for such material.

Remove all unwanted material from the blossom of trees and shrubs before pressing the flowers. Cut the backs off trumpet shaped flowers when pressing flat, but leave the bloom whole when it is being pressed in profile. When you have finished preparing the press, put the lid on and tighten down gently. At first, tighten the press daily, then less frequently until, between six and eight weeks, the plants are dry.

Once pressed, the form of a flower loses its third dimension. So when planning a design, rather than following the guidelines of three-dimensional flower arranging, you should try to create a two-dimensional representation as in a painting.

Look at the designs on the following pages and study the colour, shape and texture of each one. Then look further into the proportions, balance and rhythm of each design. Learn from the harmonizing shades and hues on page 35, the contrast of shape, colour and texture on page 31, the compelling interest — reminiscent of a 17th century painting — on page 32, the mood of cool simplicity on page 58, the delicate miniature work on page 118, and the encapsulation of the natural beauty of a meadow on page 54. And when you have copied some of these designs, maybe you will be ready to let your personal creativity take over and become an innovator of fresh ideas.

When creating your own designs, spend time choosing your flowers and foliage, carefully considering the colour and shape of each item. Consider also the size and shape of your mount or frame, and decide what shape your design is to take — the line drawings below, illustrating some basic shapes and their focal points, can be used as guidelines. Try to be confident and fix each flower straight down on to the design base rather than move it about from one place to another first — overhandling the flowers will damage their delicate structure.

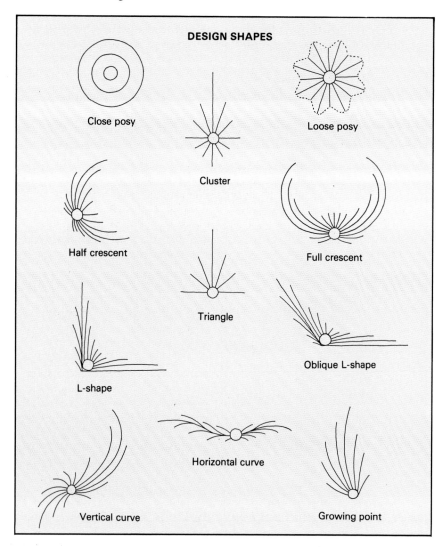

DESIGN SHAPES

Close posy

Loose posy

Cluster

Half crescent

Full crescent

Triangle

L-shape

Oblique L-shape

Horizontal curve

Vertical curve

Growing point

Pressed flower designs should always be protected to prevent damage from handling, humidity, exposure to the atmosphere and, as far as possible, from ultraviolet light. Humidity makes pressed flowers curl and exposure to air makes the colours oxidize and quickly fade. To avoid damage from ultraviolet light, which will also bleach colours, all designs should be kept away from direct sunlight, and as glass or acetate will also act as an ultraviolet filter, perhaps the most satisfactory protection is to have the design tightly sealed and covered by a sheet of glass or rigid plastic. As this is not practical in every application, other solutions have been found.

—— SEALING TECHNIQUES ——

Much of your early work will probably be in the form of greeting cards, and these require a light and flexible covering for the design. Self-adhesive, protective 'library film' is available in rolls with either a gloss or matt finish. It is easy to cut, and after some practice, to smooth over the design. Practise applying library film on a few flower groups of various thickness before you attempt a finished design. Cut a generous piece of film to cover your design, then pull away one edge of the backing paper. Position the film over the design and carefully begin to rub it down with a soft cloth, gradually pulling back the backing paper as you go. The film will need particularly careful rubbing down over thick flowers to avoid trapping air bubbles. When you have finished, trim off any excess film.

Where the greeting card involves an outer card used as a 'mount' for the inner design card, an acetate 'window' can be fixed in position over the aperture (see below), in a way that both enhances the card and protects the pressed flower design beneath.

A slightly heavier and more durable material than library film is the 'iron-on' protective film, and again this is available in gloss and matt finishes, and also in a 'linen weave' finish which is ideal for the table mat and lampshade applications (see pages 88 and 98). It is a little more expensive than the smooth-on type, and requires some practice (and not too much heat), but it does 'bond' to both flowers and base material very well and the finish gives a professional 'laminated' look.

When decorating objects such as wooden boxes or glass jars, the best way to seal the design is to cover it with several coats of varnish, either matt polyurethane or one of the new ultra hard 'two pack' types, depending on the base material. In these instances, the varnish can also be used to fix the flowers on to the design.

When covering an aperture in a greeting card, apply a line of 'impact' adhesive around the cut-out and, while it is still wet, cover with an acetate sheet.

To cover a design with protective film, gradually pull away the backing paper and rub the film down with a soft cloth, being careful to avoid air bubbles.

Items used in mounting and framing designs include picture frames, boxes with lids designed to hold craftwork, silks and satin for the design base, ribbons and lace, design papers, acetate sheets, self adhesive 'library' film, a set square, ruler and pencil, and wadding and foam sheets.

When choosing a picture frame to display pressed flower work, it is most important to make sure that the rebate in the frame (the recess which holds the glass) is deep enough to accept not only the glass, a thin mount, the design paper and the picture back, but also the wadding or foam material that is used to apply pressure to keep the flowers in contact with the glass. The picture back itself must be made of hardboard or plywood, as cardboard will not be strong enough to apply sufficient pressure. The glass must fit accurately into its frame, so that air is, to a great extent, excluded. Recommended wadding material is either synthetic wadding of the sort used in dress making, or the thin plastic foam sheeting used in upholstery. Both are equally suitable, but the depth of the rebate in the frame will decide which is best for each application.

Use wadding, as employed in dress making, to pad out frames. It can easily be cut to the correct shape, and a layer pulled off if it is too thick.

To centre the aperture on a mount, draw an 'X' on the reverse of the mount as shown, then draw your aperture with its corners touching the diagonals.

If you have decided that your picture will be enhanced by a mount, it is advisable to prepare this before starting on your design. An artist's watercolour is often set off by a rebated mount, but in a pressed flower picture, unlike a watercolour, you must have the surface of the picture pressed tightly against the glass. The material on which the design is to be made will have to be flexible enough to be pressed through the thickness of the mount by the wadding which must be cut to fit the aperture in the mount (see Victoriana on page 43). So if the design material is paper or card, the mount itself should be made of thin paper, and lines can be ruled on it to give an impression of depth (see Red Carnations on page 62).

THE FRAMING SEQUENCE

The sequence of framing a pressed flower picture depends on the material on which the flowers are being arranged. If it is paper or board, then all the framing work can be done after the picture has been completed, but if it is silk or other woven material, then all the backing material must be in place before work on arranging the flowers is started.

When working with woven material, take the picture back out of the frame and clean it carefully to remove dust and loose particles. Cut a piece of wadding and a piece of your chosen fabric just a little smaller than the back. Lay the back on your work table, centre the wadding on it, and cover with the fabric. If the picture is to have a mount around it, cut the wadding to fit the aperture. When the picture composition is complete, use a dry paint brush to clear away unwanted particles from the base material. Accurately position the mount, carefully lay the cleaned picture glass over it and then lower the frame itself over the glass. Slip your fingers under the picture back, keeping pressure on the frame, turn it over and place it on a soft surface. Now, while still keeping pressure on the back, use a small hammer to gently tack fine panel pins into the frame to hold the back in place. A heavy duty staple gun could be used, but remember that too much vibration at this stage may dislodge some of your carefully arranged flowers. Finally, use picture tape or high-tack masking tape to seal the back and cover the nail heads. Ordinary clear cellulose tape is not suitable as the adhesive dries out, it is not waterproof, and is inclined to shrink. When using rigid, rather than woven, material it is easier to pick up the finished design, lay this on top of the previously prepared wadding and picture back, and then follow the same framing procedures as described above.

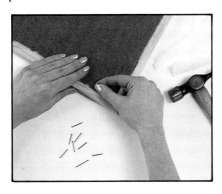

When securing the picture back, keep applying local pressure while you carefully hammer in fine panel pins every 75mm (3in).

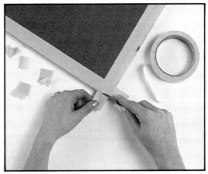

When the back is fully secured, use high-tack masking or picture frame tape to seal the gap. This excludes the air and covers the nail heads.

This beautiful design displays some of the most suitable and certainly the most colourful flowers used for pressing.

1) Russian vine 2) Fools' parsley 3) Spring flowering spiraea 4) Guelder rose
5) Whitebeam blossom 6) Blackthorn blossom 7) Meadowsweet 8) Potentilla
9) Narcissus Sol d'Or 10) Golden rod 11) Feverfew 12) Lady's mantle
13) Rose bay willow herb 14) Alyssum 15) Lobelia 16) Lady's bedstraw
17) Primrose 18) Pansy 19) Larkspur 20) Candytuft 21) Hydrangea 22) Cowslip
23) Buttercup 24) Carrot leaves 25) Melilot 26) Creeping cinquefoil 27) Kerria

28) Montbretia 29) Hop trefoil 30) Horsehoe vetch 31) Gypsophilia
32) Speedwell 33) Forget-me-not 34) Flowering currant 35) Japanese crab apple
36) Daisy 37) Heather 38) Delphinium 39) Verbena 40) Love-in-a-mist
41) Snowdrop 42) Rock rose 43) Bent grass 44) Borage 45) Cow parsley
46) Cornflower 47) Autumn flowering spiraea 48) Apple blossom
49) Creeping bent grass 50) Chervil 51) Fuchsia 52) Smoke bush

CARDS AND TAGS

A hand-made greeting card is more than just another card, it is a gift in itself — something to be kept and treasured. And, framed and mounted, any one of the delightful designs featured in this chapter would make a charming keepsake.

There are cards here to suit all occasions from Christmas and birthdays to weddings and christenings, and there is also an attractive array of gift tags that are both quick and easy to make. The chapter concludes with a couple of pretty bookmarks. You will find some helpful advice on how to make the cards themselves — as opposed to the floral designs — in the introduction on pages 15 and 19.

This card will bring your Valentine a heart 'full of flowers'. Cut a rectangle of pale blue cardboard 400mm by 200mm (16in by 8in); crease and fold it in half. With a craft knife and ruler, cut out a 128mm (5in) square from the centre of the front page. Cut four pieces of lace to fit the sides of this cut-out, mitre the corners and glue in position. Fix a square of acetate to the inside of the 'window'.

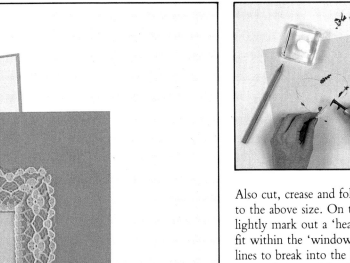

Also cut, crease and fold a white card to the above size. On the front page lightly mark out a 'heart' in pencil, to fit within the 'window', adding a few lines to break into the heart. Take a spray of *Acaena* 'Blue Haze' foliage and fix to the right hand top of the heart. Add more leaves and tendrils at various points around the shape, using only pinpoint size dots of adhesive to secure each one to the card.

Apply a tiny dot of adhesive to the top right of the heart and, using the tip of a dry, fine paint brush, tease an alyssum flower over it. Continue to fix tiny flowers all around the heart shape, finishing at the top with a forget-me-not. When the design is complete, carefully glue around the outside edge of the design card, and fix it centrally inside the blue card. Do not glue the back page down.

This traditional Christmas card is easily made. Cut a rectangle of white cardboard to measure 165mm by 65mm (6½in by 2½in). Select a piece of bracken about 140mm (5½in) in length. Fix the bracken to the card with spots of glue on the underside. Leave sufficient space at the base of this 'tree' for the 'flower pot'. For the star, colour a floret of fools' parsley gold, and glue to the top of the tree.

From red metallic board cut a rectangle 215mm by 200mm (8½in by 8in); crease, and fold in half lengthways. Now draw a rectangle — larger than the white card — on the red card using a gold marker. Cut out a 'flower pot' from some red board, draw on some decorative lines and fix the pot to the tree. Cover the design card with protective film and fix it centrally within the gold border.

Any child would be delighted to receive a pretty flower garden created in real flowers on their birthday card. From green cardboard cut a rectangle 240mm by 175mm (9½in by 7in) in size, crease it and fold it widthways. From an offcut of the green board cut out the required birthday number. Now using white cardboard cut out a rectangle 65mm by 120mm (2½in by 4¾in).

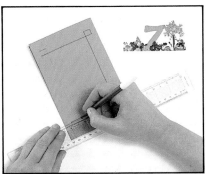

Take a large spray of meadowsweet to make the larger tree and a suitable stem for the trunk. Similarly, make a smaller tree for the other side of the number. Build up the picture by adding verbena, lobelia, cow parsley and daisies to create a colourful border. Cover the design with protective film and carefully trim to size.

Draw a border in pencil on the green card; this will house the design (the border shown is an Edwardian 'reversed corner'). When satisfied with the border, go over it with a dark green fine marker pen. Fix the design within this border.

White satin, flowers and the impression of a church steeple conveys all. Cut a piece of watercolour paper 185mm by 290mm (7¾in by 11½in); crease and fold it in half lengthways. Cut a triangle [base: 115mm (4½in), height: 145mm (6½in)] from the front of the card, then cut a single sheet of paper to fit inside the card; pencil the triangle shape on to it.

Cut 300mm (12in) of 16mm (⅝in) white satin ribbon, fold it and stick it to the apex of the triangle, leaving a loop at the top. Trim the tails to length. Cut a further 600mm (24in) and a 100mm (4in) length of ribbon. Tie a bow in the long one and form bow-like loops in the short one. Sew together and glue to the top of the triangle. Fold the ribbon ends under the card and secure.

Take the single sheet of paper and fix rose leaves and small potentillas inside the top of the triangle. Gradually add further potentillas, gypsophilia and leaves, moving down and outwards to fill the triangle. The finished look is light and spacey, giving a wedding bouquet effect. Glue a piece of acetate over the design and stick the whole sheet to the inside of the folded card.

A garland of pink alyssum and
blue forget-me-nots makes a
delightful welcome card for a new
baby. Cut and fold a blue (or pink)
and a white piece of paper to form
two cards 150mm (6in) square. Draw
and cut out a 95mm (3½in) circle
from the centre front of the coloured
card. From this circle cut out the
crib and edge it as shown with lace,
sticking the lace down with glue.

Put the white card inside the
coloured card, trim off any surplus
paper and trace a feint pencil line
through the circle on to the white
card. Put the coloured card to one
side. Glue the crib on to the centre
of the white circle, then form a
garland just inside the pencil line
using silver southernwood leaves.
Next place a cluster of pink alyssum
at the quarter points.

Scatter a few forget-me-nots to
gently break up the edge of the
clusters. Cut a 110mm (4½in)
square of white tulle and fix it using
latex adhesive on to the inside front
cover of the coloured card to cover
the hole. Finally, apply glue
sparingly all around the inside edge
of the front cover and carefully stick
the white card in position with the
design showing through the window.

This buttercup card brings a ray of sunshine with its greeting. Cut some green paper to 65mm by 165mm (2½in by 6½in). Begin the arrangement with salad burnet and melilot, placing them in the top left corner and bringing them down to form a lazy 'V'. Add buttercups towards the centre, saving the most dominant for the focal point, just off centre, at the base.

For the best effect, tuck the leaves under the focal buttercup; also ensure that the 'V' is not symmetrical. Cover the design with protective film and trim. Cut a rectangle of cream cardboard 200mm by 215mm (8in by 8½in); crease and fold it lengthways. Draw two rectangles as shown, using a green marker and making the outer rule twice as thick as the inner one. Glue the design inside the border.

Simple daisies can make a chic greeting card. Cut some pale oyster tinted cardboard to 65mm by 165mm (2½in by 6½in). Group three daisies slightly off centre, place another one a little below and to the right and a final one to the left and above the group. Fill in with leaves and stems of hedge bedstraw. Form the focal point with florets of fools' parsley positioned on the most prominent daisy.

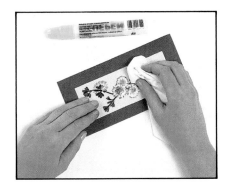

Choose purple for the main card, to match the colour with the tips of the daisy petals. Cut the card to 200mm by 215mm (8in by 8½in), score and fold lengthways into a 'tent'. Carefully cover the design with protective film and trim to size. The pale design card against the dark background card will require no border rule. Measure the central position on the background card and glue down the design.

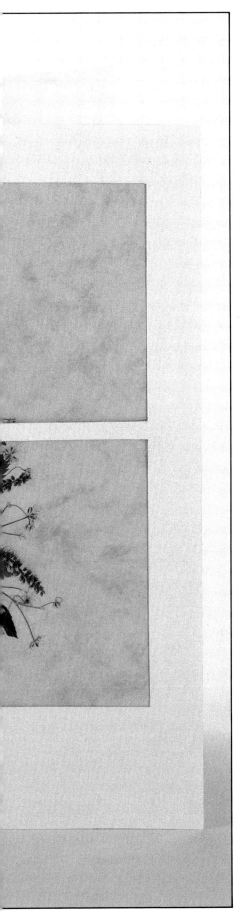

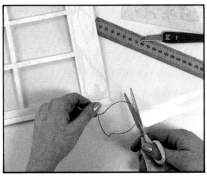

The cunning use of pink potentilla creates the beautiful illusion of a vase of roses through a window. Cut a rectangle of white cardboard 240mm by 460mm (9½in by 18in). Crease and fold it widthways. Draw a window frame on the front of the card and carefully cut it out. Cut a rectangle of acetate 230mm by 215mm (9in by 8½in) to fix inside the window, and a vase-shaped piece as shown.

Cut a single sheet of green marbled cardboard to fit inside the folded card. Arrange and secure a pyramid shape of foliage using fern, rose leaves, melilot and gypsophilia. Secure a group of uneven flower stems in the centre as shown. Cover these with the vase, fixing it at the top only, where it will be covered by further flowers and foliage. Fix potentilla and feverfew flowers (keeping the smallest at the top) over the foliage and place a sun rose in the centre. Add further sprays of foliage to drape softly over the sides of the vase. Glue the edges of the design card and fix against the acetate inside the folded card. When dry, trim off any excess green card.

The clever harmony of paper, shape and flowers gives this card a three-dimensional effect. Cut a rectangle of maroon coloured cardboard 230mm by 165mm (9in by 6½in) crease it and fold it in half widthways. Place a compass point 65mm (2½in) from the top of the card and in the centre; now draw a circle of 75mm (3in) in diameter and cut this out carefully.

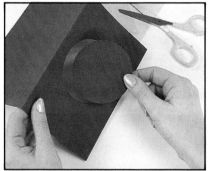

Cut and fold a sheet of grey paper (preferably imitation parchment) to fit inside the maroon card. Using a silver/mauve outline pen in the compass, describe a 56mm (2¼in) circle centrally, and 65mm (2½in) from the top of the paper, so that it will sit within the cut-out in the maroon card. Select a red potentilla, copper carpet foliage and several florets of the hebe 'Midsummer Beauty'.

On the grey paper place a spray of foliage from the centre to the top of the circle. Add more foliage at the right edge and base. Now tuck in some hebe. A potentilla at the base of the circle will form the focal point. Cut a 100mm (4in) square of acetate and fix this inside the maroon card to cover the cut-out. Glue the grey paper inside the card, to the front page, so the design is central in the aperture.

This striking design is ideal for the non flowery. Cut a rectangle from brown cardboard 207mm by 510mm (8¼in by 20in); crease and fold it widthways. Make a similar card from cream cardboard. Cut an aperture in the brown card 140mm by 190mm (5½in by 7½in). Now cut an acetate sheet to 195mm by 240mm (7¾in by 9½in) and fix it inside the brown card over the aperture.

For the design card, cut a single sheet of light brown cardboard to 190mm by 230mm (7½in by 9in). Take a selection of autumn-coloured sumach leaves and, fixing with latex adhesive, make a crab-like shape. Use leaves with curling tips to give movement to the design.

For the centre of the design, use the reverse side of an astrantia flower to show off its beautiful veining. Fix this firmly with adhesive and finally add a floret of fennel over its stalk end. Glue this design centrally to the acetate inside the aperture and when dry, glue the cream card inside the darker brown one by its front page only. Trim off any excess cream card.

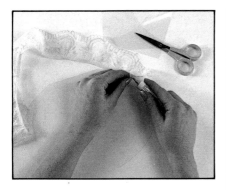

Capture the art of bygone days with this card, which can be easily converted into a calendar. From a sheet of acetate, cut an oval 180mm by 250mm (7in by 9¾in). Take one metre (about 40in) of 55mm (2½in) wide gathered cream lace, and using an 'impact' adhesive, glue the gathered edge twice around the acetate oval, about 35mm (1³/₈in) from the edge, to make a double thickness of lace.

Crease and fold in half some heavyweight dark brown cardboard. Mark out an oval on this, the same size as the acetate, but overlapping the folded edge so that, having cut the card out, the two sheets of board are joined for 90mm (3½in) at the fold. Using sprays of Russian vine and leaves of the Japanese maple *Acer palmatum dissectum,* create a crescent outline on the front cover.

Fill in the centre and the right arm of the crescent with flowers of feverfew and peach and rust coloured potentillas, and the left arm with buds and flowers of white potentilla. Now use buds and flowers of blackthorn to break up the solidness of the larger flowers. Add interest and colour to the centre with a rock geranium and a leaf of another variety of Japanese maple, *Acer palmatum atropurpurea.*

Glue around the outside edge of the front page of the brown card, and fix the acetate sheet and lace centrally over it. Leave this under pressure to dry. Finally, make a small bow from 6mm (¼in) cream satin lace and fix it to the top centre. To convert to a calendar, buy a small calendar block, cover it with brown card and trim with satin ribbon. Suspend this from the main card, then glue the card together.

The mass of gypsophilia floating up from the bed of pink alyssum gives the impression of thistledown on the breeze. This simple design makes an attractive marker for any book. Cut a strip of black cardboard 300mm by 50mm (12in by 2in). Crease a line 75mm (3in) from the top and fold under. This forms a flap to tuck over a page. Starting about 6mm (¼in) from the base, fix clusters of pink alyssum to a depth of 25mm (1in). Fill in this area with leaves of thyme. From the base build up the gypsophilia, starting with the larger flower heads, and retaining some of the stems.

Continue up the bookmark with the gypsophilia, gradually increasing the space between the flowers. Stop just under the crease line. Now add smaller gypsophilia, taking care not to fill in too much, or the airy effect will be lost. Cut a piece of protective film larger than the book mark, and carefully rub down from the base making sure not to trap any air bubbles. Trim the film flush.

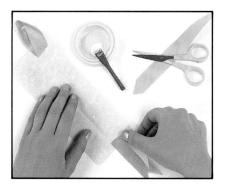

Blue delphiniums and pink candytuft are combined with mauve satin ribbon to create this most attractive bookmark. Select a piece of grey imitation parchment paper and cut a rectangle 200mm by 80mm (8in by 3¼in). Crease and fold it in half lengthways. Open up the folded parchment and on the right hand page fix a loop of 25mm (1in) wide pale mauve ribbon, using latex adhesive. Cut two pieces of ribbon 90mm (3½in) long and trim in a V-shape. Fix these to the foot of the card as shown. Turn the card over to form the design on the page opposite that bearing the ribbons.

Begin with silverweed leaves facing alternately up the page. Next fix a blue delphinium near the base and overlap with mauve candytuft. Tuck in single candytuft florets under the leaves, gradually decreasing their size up the page and finishing with a few buds. Glue the two pages of card together. Cover both sides with matt protective film (cut to the height of the bookmark and twice the width).

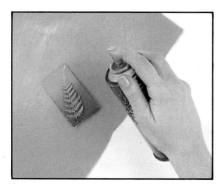

T urn offcuts of cardboard into pretty gift tags. Cut a piece each of red metallic and glossy white cardboard 75mm by 100mm (3in by 4in) and fold widthways. Secure a tip of fern to the front of the red card. Spray with gold paint and when dry, lift off the fern, leaving a red silhouette. Fix the gold fern to the front of the white card. Punch holes in the top left corners and thread with ribbon.

Cut a piece of single-sided glossy green cardboard 75mm by 100mm (3in by 4in). Crease and fold 40mm (1½in) from the left edge to give a folded card size of 75mm by 60mm (3in by 2½in). With a green marker pen, draw a border inside the larger page. Fix a spray of miniature rose leaves in one corner then form a loose line of guelder rose flowers up the page.

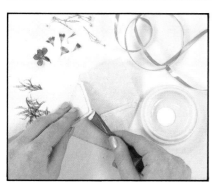

Having looked at the construction of an envelope, make a miniature version from a 140mm (5½in) square of paper. Glue the envelope together and line the side flaps with a silver marker. Take wispy foliage, gypsophilia and mauve lobelia and secure them inside the envelope so that they appear to be bursting out. Attach some curled mauve ribbon to the top of the tag.

Take some red and green single-sided cardboard and cut out some sock shapes. Using gold or silver aerosol paint, spray heads of fools' parsley; when dry, secure the best shaped florets to the heels and toes of the socks. Draw a ribbed border at the top of each sock, punch a small hole in the corner, and add coloured ties.

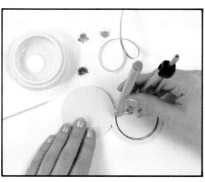

Crease and fold a small piece of yellow cardboard in half and, with your compass pencil just overlapping the fold, draw a 65mm (2½in) circle. Cut this out, leaving the card hinged together by about 30mm (1¼in) at the top. Draw a 50mm (2in) circle in green marker pen on the front cover and fix three daisies in the middle. Re-fold the card and fix a length of thin green ribbon about the fold.

—PICTURES AND PLAQUES—

Among the most satisfying and enduring items to make with pressed flowers are pictures and plaques. They make ideal gifts and you can never have too many of them in your own home. There are a variety of different styles you can create, from lacy Victorian designs such as below to stunning oriental ones (see pages 58-59). You can make pictures to commemorate a friend's or relative's anniversary or a pretty plaque to give on Mother's Day. And for that very special occasion, why not immortalize a bride's wedding day with a fabulous design made from the bride's bouquet? Details on how to mount and frame your designs can be found on pages 20-21.

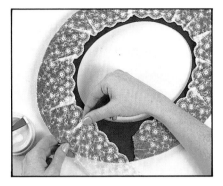

Overtones of lace and a combination of creeping vines and burgundy flowers give a Victorian flavour to this delightful design. Use an oval frame 400mm (16in) across with a burgundy mount, cut slighty wider than your chosen lace. Gather the lace around the mount, folding it at the inside edge and glueing it to the outside edge of the mount.

Cut an oval of 12mm (½in) cellulose wadding to fit exactly the centre of the mount aperture. Place the picture back face up on your bench and put the wadding in the centre. Cover this with oyster coloured silk, trimmed slightly smaller than the frame. Lay autumn leaves to form a crescent and add trails of Russian vine and fuchsia buds to break up the outline.

Add cream potentillas, fools' parsley, buds of cherry blossom and frost-tinged hydrangeas. Create a slightly solid design to give the Victorian look, then lighten the effect with the laced mount, carefully positioning the latter over the design. Next place the cleaned glass over the mount, then finish off the 'sandwich' by adding the picture frame.

Memories of a country walk will float back when you view the mixture of grasses and leaves you have gathered and prettily arranged on a sky blue background, framed in natural wood. Fresh young grass stalks, seedheads and small leaves are most suitable; make a 'growing point' using reed canary, rice, cocksfoot and quaking grasses.

Having fixed the grasses down with latex adhesive, cut off the excess stems to leave a clear space in the centre. Now fill this in with more grasses, trimming as you go. Finish at the bottom centre with a few knapweed buds and vetch foliage, to give the impression of a 'growing point'. The design is framed without a mount to give a feeling of space.

This frame, reminiscent of garden furniture, and the colourful design suggest bright summer days sitting in the garden. Select cream and brown marbled paper for the background. Fix bracken, fern and salad burnet to make an irregular fan shape, taking care not to make it symmetrical.

Use meadowsweet and yellow melilot sprays to fill in between the foliage. Now, using sprays and buds of montbretia, introduce some colour to the left of the design and put a bold spray in the bottom right corner. Create the focal point with a yellow potentilla flower nestled in amongst a large spray of hedge parsley.

Harmonize the whole arrangement by filling in with single flowers of montbretia. Now add further potentilla flowers using a palette knife to help tuck some of the petals under the hedge parsley spray. Place the cleaned glass over the completed design, turn it over and place face down in the picture frame. Add the wadding and picture back and seal it well.

Capture the beauty of that special rose. This design needs a round frame about 150mm (6in) in diameter. Cut a mount from coloured paper, then cut a white card to fit the frame. Lay the mount over the white card and very lightly pencil in the inside diameter of the mount. Take single rose leaves and fix each — slightly overlapping — with the leaf tips about 3mm (1/8in) from the pencilled circle.

Select large rose petals and repeat the process, with the top of the petals overlapping the leaves by 6mm (1/4in). Both the leaves and petals need to be fixed with very small dabs of latex adhesive. When the glue has dried, carefully rub out the pencil line and blow away the rubbings.

Now form an inner circle with smaller petals in the same way. Select the centre part of a rock rose, put a small dot of adhesive right in the middle of the rose ring, and using a palette knife, slide the rock rose centre in position. Finally, place the mount over the design card, being careful to centre it, and position the cleaned glass over both. Transfer them to the frame and secure the back.

The white and blue flowers against a dark background suggests the dawning of a new day. Select a round frame and cut a circle of blue-green cartridge paper to fit inside. Secure variegated dogwood leaves in a full crescent, with larger leaves towards the base of the crescent and smaller ones at the tips.

Place a large delphinium at the centre of the crescent. Now use lady's mantle sprays and white melilot spikes to break up the outline. Buds of feverfew and small white potentillas are added towards the ends of the crescent.

Tuck in small buds of delphinium to follow round the shape. Now use large white potentillas and small delphiniums to make an interesting strong centre, and finish the shape with a few further sprays of lady's mantle. Frame in the usual manner with light wadding or plastic foam sheeting under the frame back to provide the necessary pressure to keep the picture in place.

This beautiful ruby satin bow makes a perfect setting for specimen pressings. Take 2½m (2¾yd) of 75mm (3in) wide ribbon, and cut it into three lengths: 500mm (20in), 580mm (23in), and 1.42m (56in). Fold the shortest length, ends to centre, to form a bow and gather the centre using needle and thread. Do the same with the next longest length.

Place the smaller bow on top of the larger one, gather them tightly at the centre, and stitch together. Fold the longest length approximately in half around the centre of the double bow, and sew together at the back to form the knot of the finished bow. Also sew in a small curtain ring at the back by which to hang the design. Trim the ends of the ribbon as shown.

Cut three ovals from beige cartridge paper to fit some miniature plaques. Using a fine pen, write the botanical names of your specimens neatly at the bottom of the ovals. For the first oval, arrange stems, foliage and flowers of forget-me-not to simulate a growing plant. When satisfied with their positioning, fix down with latex adhesive and re-assemble the plaque.

For the second oval, take a large heart's ease and fix it one third of the way up from the base, then add further flowers finishing with the smallest at the top. Now introduce heart's ease leaves to give the appearance of a vigorous young plant. When satisfied, fix in position and then carefully assemble within the plaque.

Place a curved stem in the centre of the third oval and fix borage flowers and buds along the stem in a natural way so that it resembles the top of a growing stem. As before, when you have completed the picture, assemble the plaque. Take the three plaques, and arrange them down the ribbon at regular intervals. Now sew them in place, parting the ribbons slightly.

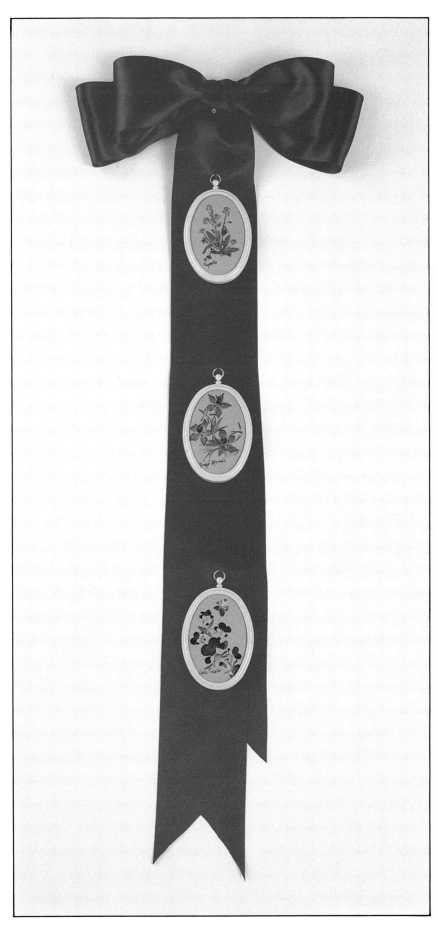

This type of compact posy has retained its popularity for the past century and would fit into any Victorian setting. Cut a piece of imitation parchment paper to fit a circular frame, and lightly pencil on it a 140mm (5½in) diameter circle. Fix tips of carrot leaves around and overlapping the circle. Now add spiraea buds and hedge parsley florets to fill out the circle.

Next take light peach coloured rose petals and fix them around and over the base of the leaves. Turn the paper in an anti-clockwise direction as each petal is secured, overlapping its neighbour, to ensure that you keep a good shape. Now secure a second row of petals over the first.

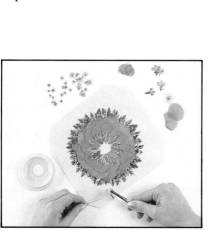

Take some variegated dogwood leaves and secure them in a circle, positioning the tips half way from the top of the second row of petals. Keep moving the card round in an anti-clockwise direction as you fix the leaves. Now fix a circle of pale blue lobelia over the dogwood.

Fix a circle of open spiraea flowers between the first and second row of rose petals, and forget-me-not and hedge parsley florets below the second row of petals. Finally, fix a ring of small rose petals within the lobelia circle and secure a cream potentilla in the centre. Cut a circular mount to fit the frame, allowing space at the perimeter of the design. Frame as usual.

Pink potentillas, highlighted against dark foliage and framed in an old gold frame, conjure up thoughts of a Victorian rose garden. Small, old frames can be found in bric-a-brac shops, and are easy to repair and paint. Cut a cream coloured rough surfaced parchment paper to fit the frame, and secure an irregular oval of red-tinged meadowsweet leaves. Place the largest pink potentilla centrally.

Fix a further six or seven mixed size potentillas with the largest at the top, interspersing them amongst the foliage to give visual depth. Make the central flower prominent by adding a few leaves under the petals. Finish by adding florets of cow parsnip to create highlights. Place the cleaned glass over the design, turn it over and put it into the frame. Put in some wadding and secure the picture back.

This design is reminiscent of early recorded flower patterns carved in Roman friezes. Choose a landscape-shaped frame about 350mm (14in) wide. Lay the picture back on a bench and cover it with thin wadding. Cut a piece of cream silk to fit the frame, and place on top. Make a soft diamond shape in carrot leaves and add small sprays of lady's mantle, using them to break up the hard outline.

Use green hydrangea florets around the outline and intersperse with small peach coloured potentillas, bringing them in towards the centre. Use larger potentillas further into the centre, tucking in extra foliage to give depth.

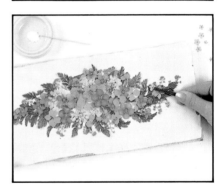

Now tuck in large heads of cream candytuft to create lightness. Finally, scatter green florets of guelder rose to relieve any solidness. Place the cleaned glass and picture frame over the design/wadding/back 'sandwich'. Slip your fingers under the picture back with your thumbs on top of the frame. Applying pressure to the sandwich, carefully turn the whole thing over and secure the back.

The new 'two pack' varnish makes it possible to seal flowers to many surfaces without altering their form or colour. Once you have mixed the varnish, you will have about two hours to complete each stage. From an art shop buy a sheet of polystyrene foam sandwiched between two lightweight sheets of drawing board. Cut a piece 230mm by 550mm (9in by 20in) with a ruler and craft knife.

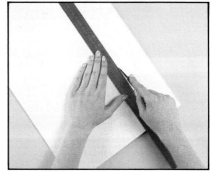

Paint on the board a pale coloured sky and field with water colour paints, and stipple them to achieve a soft effect. Set aside to dry completely.

When the background is dry, mix together a little of the two pack varnish, and apply a coat to the top two thirds of the board. Using a palette knife, start placing various grasses at intervals along the middle section of the board. The varnish will hold them in place. Use a good selection: rye grass, bearded twitch grass, brome grass, meadow fescue and squirrel tailed fescue.

Continue to build up the meadow with crested dog's tail, quaking grass, rough meadow, tufted hair, loose silky bent, hare's tail and some fennel florets. On the right hand side add yarrow leaves, fern, camomile leaves and spiraea buds to give the impression of distant trees.

Paint a thin line of varnish along the bottom 12mm (½in) and cover this with small dark green leaves to make a solid base. Re-varnish the bottom left half and fill in with more grasses, now adding common knotgrass, knapweed, shepherd's purse, speedwell, periwinkle, daisies, buttercups, lady's bedstraw, wild carrot, melilot and vetch. Now re-varnish the bottom right half.

Apply these same plants to the bottom right side. Finally, give two thin coats of varnish (allowing the first to be quite dry before applying the second) to the whole picture area. This delightful scene requires no frame, so simply fix a small ring to the back and hang it on the wall for all to admire.

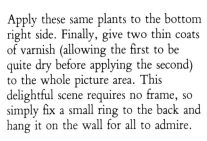

This design's 'just picked' look hides the meticulous care that is needed to make the arrangement. Use cream coloured silk for the background and a good mixture of foliage and grasses for the outline. Secure short stems at the base to represent the flower stalks. Add mixed flowers over the foliage, starting at the top with the palest colours.

Carry on down the sides of the design and then place a head of sweet cicely in the centre to cover the tops of the stems (see above). Start adding the stronger coloured flowers, fixing a large yellow *Kerria* over the sweet cicely. Finally, soften the outline by adding flowers that droop down to the base of the bunch (see below). Choose a rustic frame, pad this out and closely seal the back.

These double peonies should be picked when just open. Strip off the petals and bracts and press between layers of blotting paper, tightening the press daily. After five days change the paper, then tighten the press every three days until ready. Cut some heavy watercolour paper to 520mm by 215mm (20½in by 8½in) and arrange peony leaves in two groups as shown.

Next, fix bamboo leaf sprays, starting at one corner and curving them down towards the opposite corner. Intersperse some sprays between the peony leaf groups.

Away from the picture area, assemble the peony buds. Fix a bract on top of a small petal for the top bud, and another bract on top of two or three petals for the second bud. For the largest bud, use two bracts over four petals. Pick up the buds with tweezers and fix them in position with adhesive, tucking them under the bamboo leaves.

Create the smaller of the two open flowers in position over the ring of peony leaves as follows: using medium sized peony petals, form a ring of overlapping petals around the base of the leaves. Now add a second ring of smaller petals inside the first, and complete the flower by adding wild carrot florets to the centre.

Add a few more bamboo leaves to the large ring of peony leaves, and then use some large petals for making the irregular outer circle of the second flower. Fill in with smaller petals to make the second and third circles, and create a centre with wild carrot florets. When complete, make certain that all debris is brushed from the paper before framing the picture.

The clever use of smoke bush on green velvet helps to create a soft misty effect in this striking picture. Remove the back from a rustic frame and cover with wadding and dark green velvet. Start the design by fixing sprays of young ash tree leaves in the shape shown.

Add brown beech leaves and small buds of black knapweed to fill in the outline and create a 'bagpipe' shape.

Suggestions of the 'pipes' are represented by seed heads of pendulous sedge and bottle sedge. Add some spikes of heather to create a solid mass in the centre.

Finally soften the outline by adding the wispy flowers of smoke bush around the edges of the 'bagpipe'. When the design is complete, take care to remove all the dust and pollen from the velvet before placing the cleaned picture glass and frame over it. Slide the frame to the edge of the table and, gripping it firmly, turn it over. Apply pressure to the back of the frame, tack on and seal.

Although carnation petals press very well, they are often difficult to display. This imaginative design shows them off beautifully. Cut light blue marbled paper to fit the frame. Using the tips of ash foliage form an irregular square at the centre right, fixing the leaves with latex adhesive. Extend leaf sprays from this square to the bottom left, and form a soft curve at the top right.

Use individual petals of red carnation to build up a large flower over the square of leaves (see above). Make smaller flowers above and below this, and a couple of buds using two or three petals together. Finally, follow the curve with heads of wild carrot (see below). Place a mount (made from darker blue paper) over the design, having first drawn a fine line around its inside edge. Frame as usual.

Here's a charming way to provide the bride with an everlasting memento of her wedding day. And there should be plenty of flowers left over to make gifts for other special guests as well, including yourself! See overleaf for the bride's picture and on the following pages for guidelines to making the other designs: 28, 47, 50, 62, 80 and 97.

If you intend to press the bouquet, ensure the florist does not spray the flowers. Seal the bouquet as soon as possible in a dry plastic box on a bed of tissue paper and keep it in a cool place until you are ready to press it — preferably the next day. Dismantle the bouquet by carefully unwiring each item then press the flowers as described on page 17, leaving them under increasing pressure for six weeks.

Mask a photograph of the bouquet to match the shape of your chosen frame — this will help you to follow the bouquet's design more easily. Lay the picture backing on your work surface and cover it with paper, wadding and ivory silk, cut to size. Using latex adhesive to fix the flowers, copy the shower trail. Make the rosebuds from a few small petals and a couple of sepals.

Now build up the outline with the foliage, moulding the shape to fit comfortably into the frame. Using the photograph as reference, add flowers and buds to the design. Form carnation buds with a few sepals to several petals.

Continue to add more flowers and leaves. If you are using polyanthus, you will find the flowers appear very thin after pressing, so place one on top of another to give greater depth. Using some coloured ribbons saved from the bouquet, stick three short lengths together, and add two loops to form a bow. Fix this in position on one side of the bouquet and add a short length to the other side.

Make up some rosebuds as before and use these to fill in the centre of the design along with some foliage and other flowers; used here are polyanthus, carnation and gypsophilia.

Make a large open rose by arranging a ring of small overlapping petals on top of a large base petal. Fix sepals to the back of the rose so that they extend beyond the petals and bed the flower in the centre of the design. When complete, frame the picture as usual. The remaining flowers, together with the bridesmaids' bouquets, can be used to make gifts for other members of the wedding party.

This picture is a charming way to mark a 25th anniversary. Choose a 250mm (10in) square silver picture frame with a 150mm (5¾in) mount. Cut a 230mm (9in) square of textured water colour paper and, with a silver marker pen in your compass, draw a series of circles of varying thickness to fit within the mount. Draw the number '25' on to a piece of tracing paper, and transfer this to the circle.

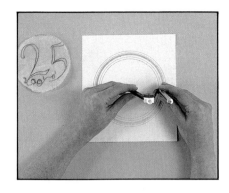

Use very small flowers to fill in the numbers: forget-me-not, thyme, candytuft, lady's mantle, melilot, and red, yellow and purple alyssum. For the tiniest flowers, apply glue directly on to the card and tease the flowers into position with a paint brush. Larger flowers can have the glue applied directly to their backs using a toothpick.

Having completed the numbers, link them at the base with sprays of mind-your-own-business leaves and hawthorn blossom. Centre the design card within the mount, and fix with masking tape. Cover the whole thing with the cleaned picture glass and frame, and turn it over. Now insert some wadding. Replace the picture back and, while under pressure, tack it in place. Seal with masking tape.

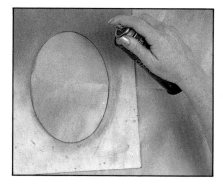

The charm and tranquility of bygone days are remembered with favourite flowers preserved in an old golden frame — a perfect gift for a 50th wedding anniversary. Old picture frames can easily be found in bric-a-brac shops and can be quickly revived with a spray of gold paint. Newer frames can be 'aged' by also spraying both frame and mount with 'old gold' spray paint.

Cut a piece of wadding the same size as the aperture in the mount, and lay it on the picture back. Cover with dark brown silk, cut to the size of the frame, and make an impression of the mount on the silk. Begin with flowers of 'Blazing Star' bartonia, fixing them in the centre, with the largest on top. Now add rock geranium leaves, keeping the smallest ones towards the edge.

Add a spray of meadowsweet to the bottom left and fill in elsewhere with individual flowers. Add a few hazel catkins for interest. Lift the edge of the largest bartonia flower with a palette knife, slip a couple of rust coloured geum flowers half under it, and add a third to its left edge for balance. Finally, soften the edges with seedheads of creeping bent grass. Mount and frame as usual.

A silver cross combined with a simple but dignified design and mounted into a silver wall plaque makes a perfect gift for a baptism or confirmation. These wall plaques are available at many craft shops. Open up the plaque and cut out some grey marbled or imitation parchment to fit. Mark out a cross on grained silver paper, cut it out and fix it centrally on to the grey paper.

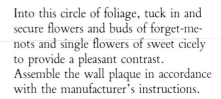

Form a 'crown of thorns', using narrow leaf sprays of lady's bedstraw. Place each spray in a circle around the junction of the cross, using a palette knife to easy each spray into position. Fix with tiny spots of latex adhesive. Turn the paper as you proceed to make this task easier.

Into this circle of foliage, tuck in and secure flowers and buds of forget-me-nots and single flowers of sweet cicely to provide a pleasant contrast. Assemble the wall plaque in accordance with the manufacturer's instructions.

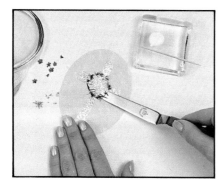

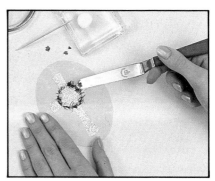

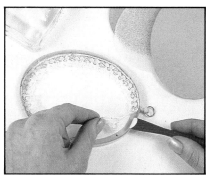

'M' is for mother, made with flowers, and this is a gift she will always treasure. Purchase a pink wall plaque from a craft shop. Take the frame, turn it over and fix some fine lace inside the rim with latex adhesive. Mark out and cut some pink cartridge paper to fit the plaque.

Mark out lightly in pencil a large 'M' on the pink paper. Cover the letter with stems and small leaves of common burnet, forget-me-not buds and small grasses, securing them with tiny dots of latex adhesive. Use a curved spray of *Acaena* 'Blue Haze' to create the 'serifs' at the top and foot of the letter.

Build up over this outline with single flowers of pink, yellow and purple alyssum and slivers of pink cornflower petals. Finally, add extra foliage to balance the design and place a miniature heart's ease at the centre of the 'M'. Follow the manufacturer's instructions to assemble the plaque.

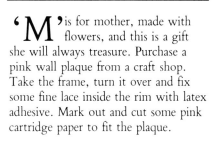

-BOXES AND PAPERWEIGHTS-

$\mathbf{B}$oxes of all shapes and sizes can be decorated with pressed flowers to make that perfect gift. The designs on boxes such as the wooden one shown below need to be protected with a coat of varnish, but you can also buy an attractive range of boxes and pots from craft shops and mail order craft suppliers that have specially designed airtight lids to protect your arrangement. A selection of such pots has been used in this chapter, each incorporating an attractive floral design to complement the colour, size and shape of the pot. A variety of glass paperweights can also be bought from craft suppliers and here you will find four imaginative ways to decorate them.

The colours and fine grain of this beautiful cherrywood box are complemented by the subtle arrangement of autumnal foliage. Begin by creating an 'L' shaped outline with leaves of Japanese maple, autumn cherry, willow, wayfaring tree, hawthorn, sumach and smoke bush.

Continue adding the foliage, using sufficient adhesive to fix each leaf securely. Trim any overlapping pieces, so as to avoid excess bulkiness. When you are happy with the shape, coat it with a thin layer of matt varnish.

Now add small buds of blue lobelia, creating a sweeping curve throughout the outline. Use larger, open flowers in a cluster at the left and base of the design to form the focal point. Finish with two thin coats of varnish.

The rich leaves of the Norway maple are ideally suited to the tone of this walnut box, their colour and texture creating a marquetry effect. Sand the box and coat with a thin layer of matt varnish. Place leaves of the Norway maple 'Goldsworth Purple' on to the lid to form an open cluster and leave to dry. The varnish will be sufficient to hold the leaves in place.

When the first layer of varnish is completely dry, apply a second coat. Place a few pale pink larkspur flowers and buds over the top right of the leaf cluster.

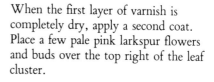

At the opposite corner, position a large head of common water dropwort over the maple leaves. Fill in the outline with open larkspur flowers, then tuck individual florets of water dropwort along the bottom of the larkspur. When dry, finish with two thin coats of varnish.

Black forms a chic backdrop for many pale plants. Here, the pale blue and eau-de-nil colours sit very prettily. Begin by coating the lid of a small black box with special 'two pack' gloss varnish. Place sprays of mugwort leaves, underside uppermost, in the left hand corners.

Add two mugwort sprays to the right hand corners. Now, carefully splitting a leaf spray, create a fan shape in the top centre of the lid.

Just below the fan, in the centre of the box, form a small cluster of mugwort leaves and, on top, fix a little arrangement of blue lobelia and cornflower florets. Seal the design with two thin coats of varnish.

A HEART FULL OF FLOWERS

This heart shaped trinket box makes a pretty gift for someone you love. Cut a heart shaped piece of ivory silk to fit the lid. Now cut 75mm (3in) of 6mm (¼in) wide ivory satin ribbon. Fold the ribbon in half, trim each end and glue to a small geranium leaf. Fix this near the point of the heart as shown.

Fix another leaf on top of the fold in the ribbon and then add leaves alternatively to the right and the left, building up a heart shaped outline. When the shape is complete, fix florets of cow parsley over the inner edge of the leaves.

Fill the centre of the heart with rich red verbena. Finally, fix a small ivory satin bow to the top of the heart as shown below and assemble the box lid according to the manufacturer's instructions.

A nother pretty design for a trinket box lid. Cut an oval from pale green cardboard to fit the lid. Form a full crescent shape outline with sprays of miniature rose leaves and hairy tare.

Now follow the outline with tendrils and buds of vetch. For the focal point, choose an open peach potentilla and fix it to the base of the crescent, slightly off centre.

With the aid of a palette knife, tuck a green hydrangea floret under the right side of the focal flower. Add a few small guelder roses and slip a second potentilla between the foliage. To complete the design tuck another hydrangea floret and a third potentilla into the design just above the focal flower to balance the arrangement. Assemble the lid as instructed by the manufacturer.

The dramatic effect of white flowers against a black silk background enhances the silver plated trinket box to create a sophisticated gift. These trinket boxes can be readily purchased from craft shops. Open up the lid assembly and take out the foam padding. Cut a circle of black silk to cover the padding.

Secure sprays of miniature variegated rose leaves in a crescent shape. Now add sprays and single flowers of gypsophilia, tucking the stems under the leaves where necessary.

Starting at the tips of the crescent, and building to the centre, add buds and flowers of feverfew. Place a large full flower of feverfew towards the bottom centre to create a focal point. When the design is complete, cover it with the plastic sheet from the lid, and assemble according to the manufacturer's instructions.

Once you have gained confidence in using larger flowers, you will find this miniature design an exciting challenge. Buy a miniature crystal bowl (available from good craft shops) and use the white card from its lid as the design card. Start by fixing the tiny foliage of shepherd's purse in place to make a full crescent outline.

Fill in the outline with florets of yellow and pink alyssum and elder flower. To fix the flowers in position first place a tiny spot of latex adhesive in the required place and, using a paint brush, gently tease a flower over it, then press it to secure.

Finally, tuck in heart's ease, keeping the largest to make a focal point towards the bottom centre of the design. Place the plastic circle from the lid over the finished design, and assemble according to the maker's instructions.

This attractive arrangement of ruby coloured flowers makes a perfect gift for a 40th wedding anniversary. Purchase a crystal bowl from a good craft shop. Take the padding foam from the lid and cut a piece of ivory coloured silk to cover it. Start fixing to this, with small applications of adhesive, sprays of *Acaena* 'Blue Haze' and miniature rose leaves to form a full crescent.

When pressed and dried, potentilla 'scarlet' flowers assume a rich ruby colour, and are very suitable for this design. Place a potentilla flower at the base of the crescent, just left of centre; working from this, fix further potentillas around the circle as shown.

Touch a small amount of adhesive to the base of several florets of the hebe 'Midsummer Beauty', and carefully tuck them under the edges of the foliage to add colour. Finally, intersperse flowers of blackthorn and florets of fools' parsley to balance the design. Reassemble the lid according to the manufacturer's instructions.

This is a simple but elegant way to use empty gift boxes as containers for pot-pourri. We have selected a green and a black box. Take the lid off one of the boxes and lightly secure three whole flower heads of cow parsley diagonally across it. With aerosol spray paint, give the top of the box two light coats of gold paint.

When the paint is dry, remove the parsley to reveal the unsprayed part of the box. This shows up as a pretty pattern through the paint. Now fix the gold sprayed cow parsley to the other box lid. These boxes are filled with 'Noel' pot-pourri, which is a festive mixture of small cones, tree bark and citrus peel. Cover the pot-pourri with cling film (plastic wrap) before replacing the lids.

Not every arrangement need be pretty and feminine. This design is perfect for any man's desk. Cut a piece of cardboard to fit the recess of the paperweight and place a thin layer of latex adhesive along one edge. Fix to the strip of adhesive a selection of leaves, overlapping each other and the edge. Repeat for the other three sides then trim the leaves flush with the side of the cardboard.

Fill in the centre of the design with smaller leaves. Shown here are hawthorn, virginia creeper, flowering cherry, spiraea, *Euonymus*, smoke bush, and *Acaena* 'Copper Carpet'. Overlap the foliage randomly to create a more natural appearance.

When the design is complete, fit it into the recess of the paperweight. If necessary, pad out with foam before sealing with the self-adhesive baize supplied.

If you don't feel up to scripting the words for this design, see if you can locate a caligrapher or illustrator to do it for you. Cut the paper on which the words are inscribed to fit into the paperweight's recess. Surround your quotation or verse with several sprigs of thyme foliage.

Intersperse the foliage with a pretty range of minute flowers: shown here are spiraea, forget-me-not, red alyssum, star of Bethlehem, buds of Japanese crab, thyme and melilot. To fix each flower, put a dot of latex adhesive in the required place on the design card and tease the flower into position with a paintbrush; press lightly to secure.

To complete the design add a few buds and flowers of the hebe 'Simon Delux' and some yellow alyssum. Finally, place a heart's ease to the right of the verse before fitting the design into the paperweight and sealing it with the self-adhesvie baize supplied.

Commemorate a special event with this highly individual paperweight. Cut a circle of white cardboard to fit inside the recess of the paperweight. Divide the circle into eight equal segments using a fine pencil, then draw a 25mm (1in) gold circle in the centre. Outline the circle inside and out with a black pen and mark out the segments with gold.

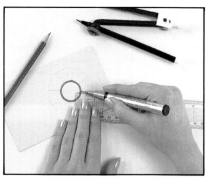

Inside the centre circle write the date that you wish to commemorate with a black pen. Now form a background on each segment with small sprays of yarrow foliage. Secure them with the stems toward the centre.

On two opposite segments place several buds of pale pink candytuft and an open flower at the centre. In the opposing segments use single flowers of yellow melilot, red alyssum and segments of sweet cicely. Put the design inside the paperweight recess and pad out with foam if necessary. Seal the design with the self-adhesive baize supplied.

Astunning design for that special birthday is easily created with a few flowers. Begin by cutting a black card to fit the oval recess of the paperweight. Paint the figure '21' in white to the right of the oval.

Break up mugwort foliage and, keeping the white underside uppermost, fit it to the card following the outline of the oval. Where the foliage meets the '21', add some budded sprays of gypsophilia.

Intersperse a few open flowers of gypsophilia amongst the foliage then create the focal point with a large open flower of white larkspur. To complete the design, tuck a small larkspur flower under the leaves above the focal point, and place a larkspur bud below. Position the design card inside the recess of the paperweight, pad out with foam if necessary, and seal with the self-adhesive baize supplied.

—DECORATIVE TABLEWARE—

Flowers in one form or another always make a colourful addition to the dinner table and pressed flowers are no exception. So why not brighten up your next dinner party with one of the delightful designs featured in this chapter? There are inexpensive and easy-to-make place cards suitable for all occasions — including weddings — an attractive place mat, candles, a candlestick holder, and a lovely ribbon napkin tie. And for those prepared to spend a little more money on specialist craft items, there are also drinks coasters, napkin rings and a tray (shown below), all imaginatively decorated with a beautiful range of flowers.

Afternoon tea takes on real elegance with this striking tray purchased from craft suppliers. Fix a cluster of autumn plumbago leaves at one end of the oval card (supplied with the tray) and at the other end fix a smaller cluster of plumbago and autumn wild strawberry leaves. Now enlarge and fill out these two clusters with leaf sprays of *Acaena* 'Blue Haze'. Keep each cluster fairly oval in shape.

Working first on the smaller cluster, create a focal point with a red-tinged green hydrangea flower sitting on top of a wild carrot head. Now form a gentle curve of pink potentilla across the top of the cluster and finish off with green hydrangea and red saxifrage. For the focal point of the larger cluster place a deep red potentilla on top of a head of wild carrot.

To add depth, tuck some pink potentilla and red-tinged hydrangea under the carrot head. Now place two smaller 'Red Ace' potentillas above the focal point. Make a gentle diagonal curve into the centre of the design with buds of Japanese crab apple and finish off with sprays of greyhair grass. Reassemble the tray according to the manufacturer's instructions.

An ingenious idea which adds individuality to any table setting. Begin by cutting a rectangle of hardboard 215mm by 280mm (8½in by 11in). Round off the corners with sandpaper. Next, cut a piece of green marbled paper to fit the hardboard. Draw two double-lined borders with green pen in opposite corners, as shown.

Using foliage of the *Ranunculus* 'Bachelor's Buttons', make a triangular shape in the top left corner and an 'L' shape in the bottom right. Add fuchsias to the triangle, beginning with a bud at the apex, gradually adding more open flowers and finishing at the widest part with a full flower. Repeat the process on the 'L' shape, using fuchsia buds at the tips and a full flower in the centre.

Seal the design with a transparent linen-surface covering — the type that is ironed on. Trim the edges. Now cover the back of the design card with latex adhesive and fix carefully on to the hardboard. Finally, fix a rectangle of green felt on to the reverse side of the table mat.

These glass drinks coasters — easily available from craft shops — lend themselves to a carnation display. Cut a circle of moss green cartridge paper to fit into the recess of the large bottle coaster. Now fix large petals of yellow carnation, overlapping them slightly, to form an outer circle.

Fill in the outer circle with smaller carnation petals to create a second circle. Small petals from the centre of the carnation make up the final inner circle. To complete the display fix cow parsley florets to the centre.

Fit the design card into the recess of the bottle coaster and seal with the circle of baize supplied. Repeat this process for each drinks coaster, using different colours for an attractive display.

Select a colour to complement the bride's attendants and these place cards will enhance the wedding feast. Cut a rectangle of cardboard 170mm by 65mm (6½in by 2½in); crease and fold it widthways. Select some grained silver paper and, using a template, mark and cut out an oval 37mm by 55mm (1½in by 2¼in). Trim the silver paper to 55mm by 75mm (2¼in by 3in), keeping the oval centred.

Glue the silver paper cut-out centrally to the front of the card using a glue pen. With latex adhesive, fix some carrot leaves in a crescent shape at the top right corner, and slightly smaller ones to the bottom left. Place a small head of fools' parsley centrally on each crescent.

Build up on these corner designs with pink candytuft florets and more pieces of fools' parsley to give an elegant balance.

The combination of cream coloured blossom and lace prettily complement traditional china at the dinner table. Cut a rectangle of dark brown cardboard 110mm by 80mm (4½in by 3¼in). Crease and fold it widthways to form a 'tent'. Using a gold marker pen carefully write the desired name in the centre of the top page.

Take about 300mm (12in) of cream lace and, starting about three quarters of the way along the folded edge, fix it to the card with a little latex adhesive. Pinch the lace to form gathers as you round the corners and fix with a little extra adhesive.

Using the buds and open flowers of blackthorn, make an 'L' shape at the top right corner. Use an open flower to cover the join in the lace. Create the focal point by using a pair of open flowers, glued one on top of the other. This will also give these delicate flowers greater depth. Make a similar shape, but without the focal point, at the bottom left corner.

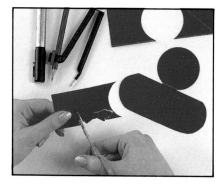

This pretty place card provides a warm welcome to the Christmas table. Using single sided red metallic cardboard, first draw a rectangle 50mm by 125mm (2in by 5in), and then a 50mm (2in) diameter circle centrally above it, with the edges overlapping. Cut this out carefully, rounding off the short ends of the rectangle to make a 'lozenge' shape. Cut out a small 'bow' from the offcut.

Add details to the bow with a gold marker pen. Now draw a gold line all around the 'lozenge', about 5mm (¼in) from the edge. Turn the card over and write the desired name in the centre of the white circle with a black pen. Highlight the letters with the gold marker pen.

Fold the card so that the red side of the base, and the white side of the circle, are uppermost. Using latex adhesive, and starting at the top right centre of the circle, fix fern pieces, leaves of salad burnet and stamen of astrantia to form a garland. Make sure the garland is balanced, and touch in some gold highlights with the marker pen.

Capture the freshness of warm summer days with an easily made daisy chain place card. Cut a rectangle of yellow cardboard 100mm by 85mm (4in by 3¼in). Crease and fold it widthways. Write the desired name in the centre of the front page with a green marker pen.

Create an oval border around the name with stems of daisies, leaving room between them to place the daisy flowers. Finish off the oval at the base with a gently curving stem and daisy bud.

Now fix open daisy heads between the stems, making sure that there are no gaps between flowers and stems. Link the bottom bud with a further bud to complete the daisy chain. The largest daisy should be placed at the top centre to give balance to the design.

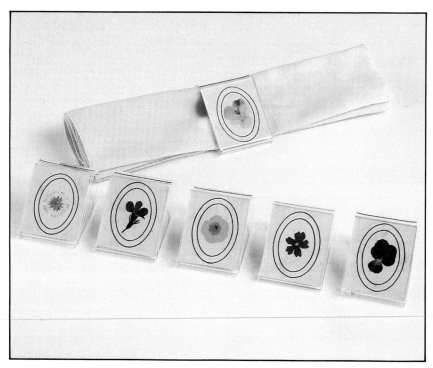

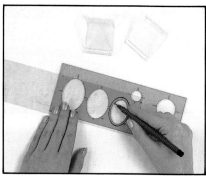

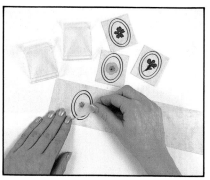

Those simple but attractive napkin rings can be purchased from craft suppliers and make a perfect complement to any dinner party. On a strip of green marbled cardboard, mark out an oval 50mm by 37mm (2in by 1¼in) with a green pen. Inside this oval, mark out a smaller one, also in green. You will need a template to achieve an accurate shape.

Repeat this procedure using a wide range of different coloured flowers; used here are buttercup, blue lobelia, daisy, red verbena and different varieties of pansy.

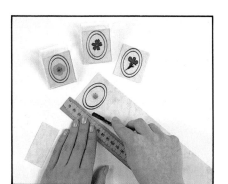

In the centre of the ovals, fix an attractive flowerhead. Cover the design with protective film, smoothing out any air bubbles. With the aid of a steel rule and craft knife, trim the strip to fit the napkin holder.

This napkin holder offers a delightful alternative to the standard napkin ring. Cut 1½m (5ft) of 40mm (1½in) wide peach satin ribbon. About 100mm (4in) from one end fix a peach potentilla. Tuck melilot foliage above and below this, then add three spikes of white melilot above. Arrange an identical display about 50mm (2in) from the other end of the ribbon.

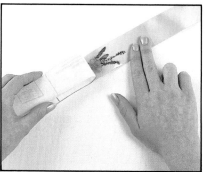

Cut two strips of protective film, about 200mm (8in) long, and cover the ends of the ribbon. Firmly stroke out any air bubbles. Trim the ends of the ribbon into 'V' shapes. Finally, tie the ribbon into a generous bow around a triangular napkin arrangement, allowing one end to fall slightly longer than the other, as shown.

A plain wooden candlestick can be decorated very effectively with pressed flowers. Begin by coating the candleholder with 'two pack' gloss varnish. While the varnish is still tacky, adhere sprays of *Ranunculus* 'Bachelor's Buttons' foliage to both back and front of the holder. Leave to dry.

Re-varnish the holder and centre a spray of montbretia buds on top of the foliage (see above). Add larger, single buds towards the base. While this second coat of varnish is still sticky, fix a cream potentilla in the centre of each design (see below). Leave the holder to dry completely before finishing with two thin coats of gloss varnish.

BY CANDLELIGHT

These delicate designs transform ordinary thick candles. But be very careful not to let the candle burn down below the protective film, as the designs are not flameproof! For the yellow candle fix three autumn sumach leaves in a spray with latex adhesive. Repeat twice around the candle.

The other candle is offset with five pink larkspur flowers fixed around the base. Rue leaves are tucked in and around the flowers. Finally, add some larkspur buds a little above the foliage. Carefully cover the designs on both candles with protective film, allowing an extra 5mm (¼in) above the design. Rub the film down carefully and avoid trapping any air bubbles.

—GIFTS AND NOVELTIES—

It can be great fun to break away from the more conventional types of pressed flower designs — pictures, cards, boxes and so forth — and, instead, look around the home for more unusual objects to decorate, such as book ends, letter racks, old storage jars, notebooks, sunglasses, lampshades and even furniture. As this chapter shows, all these things and many, many more can be transformed with an attractive and complementary floral design and these novelties make such delightful gifts.

For further gift ideas, there is a selection of attractive costume jewellery — some to be made at no great cost — and there is also a charming little perfume pot, complete with recipe for the solid perfume.

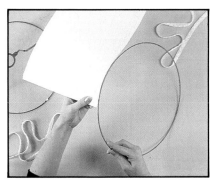

The unique marking and leaf formation of love-in-a-mist make an eye-catching design on a plain white lampshade. Make certain that the shade you use is of the type that has a paper or similar rigid backing to its fabric. Take it apart carefully and lay the material out to flatten. Select about eight each of small, medium and large sized love-in-a-mist flowers.

Spread out the material from the shade and lay the flower heads on it, with smaller flowers at the top and larger ones at the base. Make sure that no flower is at the same level as its immediate neighbours. When you have the right effect, turn the flowers over one at a time, apply latex adhesive to the centre and tips of the sepals and fix down securely in position.

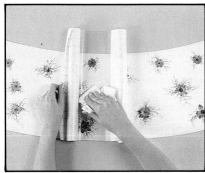

Cover the design with semi-matt, canvas textured, iron-on protective film. Cut a generous strip of film, mark the centre line in pencil and roll it up from both ends towards the centre. Carefully cut along the centre line through backing paper only then slowly peel off one side of backing, smoothing down the film as you go. Repeat for the other side. Iron on the film and reassemble the shade.

Feverfew flowers and rose leaves transform a simple letter rack into a handsome writing table accessory. Start by coating the front face of the bottom rack with matt varnish. Place a spray of rose leaves on the left hand side, pointing upwards from the bottom corner. Add a feverfew bud just above the first leaf and a flower at the end of the spray.

Position a second rose leaf spray next to the first, this time pointing it downwards. Continue in this way across the rack, adding feverfew flowers between the sprays. When the design is dry, give two further coats of thin varnish. Follow the whole procedure once again for the top rack.

Once again, a plain wooden container is enhanced by the addition of a few flowers. Begin by varnishing the front of the utensil holder. With a palette knife gently ease into position an oval outline of feverfew foliage.

Starting at the top of the outline, fill in with buds of feverfew, gradually working down the design with both buds and flowers. Finish at the base of the foliage with the largest feverfew flowers to create a focal point. Tuck in extra leaves to fill any gaps and when the design is dry, finish with four further coats of varnish.

Plain pine book ends can easily be decorated using a selection of pressed flowers. Begin by painting one book end with matt varnish. While the varnish is still sticky, create a loose triangular shape, starting with a miniature rose leaf spray and buds of blue delphinium.

Working in gentle curves, position peach potentillas to the left and delphiniums to the right of the design. Scatter spiraea 'Snowball' florets throughout, and finish by extending the outline with a few small leaves. When dry, coat the design again with two thin coats of matt varnish.

COAT RACK

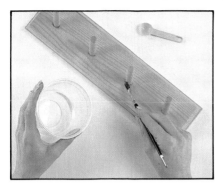

Russian vine is a natural creeper, so it is in an ideal setting, creeping and climbing over this pine coat rack. First, sand the wood thoroughly before applying one coat of 'two pack' varnish.

With the aid of a palette knife, start to adhere sprays of Russian vine to the varnish, putting them at various heights along the length of the rack. Add a few leaves and single sprays to fill in.

Cover the vine stem ends as you go with the feathery foliage of camomile. When the design is complete, and the varnish dry, apply two further coats of varnish.

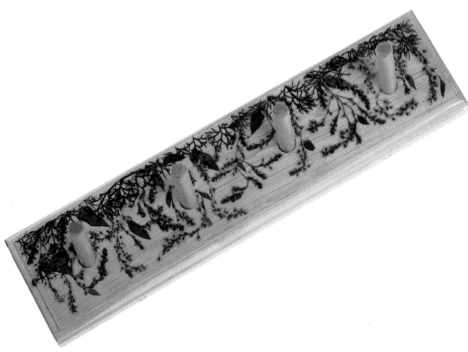

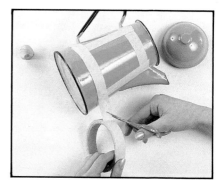

Blue lobelia is an attractive addition to plain yellow enamel. Start by marking out a rectangular area on the side of the pot with masking tape. Now lay the pot on its side, securing it to your work surface with an adhesive putty such as Blu-Tack. Paint the area with a thin coat of 'two pack' varnish. Take care the varnish does not build up at the tape edge and form a ridge.

While the first coat of varnish is still sticky, position several carrot leaves to form a teardrop shape outline. When this design is completely dry, add another coat of varnish.

Now, fill in with the flowers. Use lobelia, beginning with buds at the top and coming down to the base with larger flowers. Fill in any gaps with foliage and add a couple of budded stems at the base to create a natural effect. When this is dry, remove the tape and give a final coat of varnish, feathering the edges by wiping them with a lint-free cloth.

This type of white enamel canister can be bought either new or second hand. Secure the canister to your work surface with blobs of adhesive putty. Now take a large head of mauve candytuft and fit to the centre of the canister with latex adhesive. Surround the flower with salad burnet leaves and add two more candytuft flowers on either side. Paint over the design with 'two pack' varnish.

For the canister lid, coat with varnish before positioning a circle of salad burnet leaves — slightly apart — around the knob. Fill in between the leaves with large, single candytuft flowers. When dry, seal this design with two thin coats of varnish, feathering the edges with a lint-free cloth.

This his plain black address book is enhanced by the addition of white flowers. Take 17 buds of white larkspur and trim the largest one square at its base. Fix this to the book cover, about 12mm (½in) from the bottom edge. Add a little larkspur foliage to give the appearance of a growing base. Now select the next two largest buds and fix them above the first bud.

Now fix larkspur buds of decreasing size, with some stem attached, in pairs up the page — one facing one way and the next the other. Make certain that the buds are all different heights. Cut a piece of matt protective film the height of the book, plus a 25mm (1in) overlap, and the width of the design, plus 12mm (½in). Rub down carefully, turning in the overlap on all three sides.

This inexpensive notebook is given individuality and style by the addition of pressed flowers. First hide the name plate on the front cover with *Euonymus* 'Emerald 'n' Gold' leaves. Fixed them in place randomly to give a natural looking posy, adding autumn coloured leaves of chervil.

Next, fix whole heads of pink and purple candytuft, overlapping them to create a solid effect. Finally, cut a square of matt protective library film, large enough to cover the design with a margin of about 5mm (¼in) beyond the outermost flowers. Peel off the backing paper and rub down the film in position, taking care not to trap any air bubbles.

A series of carrot flowerheads arranged around a terracotta plant pot creates an unusual mossy effect. Begin by coating one half of the pot with matt varnish. Place a double row of wild carrot flowerheads around this side of the pot.

Once one half of the pot is complete, repeat this procedure on the other half. When the design is finished, cover the whole pot with two thin coats of matt varnish.

T his novel idea identifies any plants which have been sown as seeds. These attractive and useful items make perfect gifts for the keen gardener, too. Buy a pack of plastic markers from a garden nursery and cover several with a coat of matt varnish.

Selecting a range of suitable flowers, begin placing one flowerhead at the top of each marker. When the varnish is dry, paint the markers with two further coats of varnish.

If you are making these for yourself you obviously need to use flowers that you intend to grow from seed. For a gift, suggested flowers as shown here include heart's ease, blue and mauve lobelia, forget-me-not, and purple and red alyssum.

This pretty chalet-style chair is child size, but you can just as easily create the design shown here on a full scale chair. Lay the chair down on to your work surface and coat the front of the top rung with 'two pack' varnish. Now form a wavy garland using the trailing stems of 'mind-your-own-business' plant, leaving a gap in the middle. In between the leaves place single florets of red alyssum.

When dry, apply another thin coat of varnish in preparation for the next flowers. Now varnish the lower rung. Place a large red alyssum in the centre and add a short trail of mind-your-own-business to the left. At the end of this trail add another, smaller head of alyssum, before finishing with just a few mind-your-own-business leaves. This forms half the garland. Repeat on the right side.

Now return to the top rung. Place three rose leaves in the centre of the garland, and add a small spray of cow parsley and florets of red alyssum to the tip of each leaf.

Position a single larkspur bud at either end of the garland. Now take two medium sized larkspur flowers and place them equidistant from the centre, at the high points of the garland. Finish with a large pink larkspur in the centre. The completed design is shown below on a larger scale to help you see more detail.

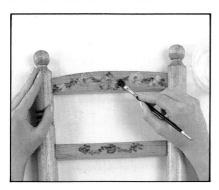

When both rungs have dried completely, apply two or three coats of varnish to seal the designs. Be quite sure that each coat is dry before applying the next.

These specially designed door plates, available from craft suppliers, can be decorated to suit the decor of any room. Cut a piece of protective film to cover the back of the plate and a piece of foam to fit the centre of the plate without overlapping the holes. Then cut a rectangle of coloured cardboard to fit the recess and punch holes in the corners to match those in the plate.

Create the design above with the narcissus 'Sol d'Or' and tiny florets of cornflower. Place the design card in the recess at the back of the plate, pad out with the foam and seal the back with protective film. The design below is made with sprays of montbretia buds, autumn leaves and potentilla. The third example contains specimens of meadowsweet, buttercup and cowslip.

A gold pendant makes a delightful setting for a delicate cream and brown design. Cut an oval of brown cardboard to fit, then select small cream buds and flowers of traveller's joy and hawthorn, and sprays of autumn coloured *Acaena microphylla* leaves. Form a soft crescent of leaves, placing dots of adhesive directly on to the card and teasing each leaf into place with a paintbrush.

Now add buds of traveller's joy and sprays of *Acaena* to complete the full crescent shape, using a toothpick to place the adhesive directly on to the back of the larger flowers.

Place a large hawthorn flower at the base of the design and highlight it by tucking flowers of traveller's joy under the petals. Fill in the crescent with the remaining smaller hawthorn flowers. Reassemble the pendant, taking care that when it is sealed the design card is packed tight under the glass.

This exquisite piece of matching jewellery simply needs a little patience to complete. Cut a white cardboard oval to fit the brooch and fix sprays of miniature maidenhair fern to create a flowing outline. Scatter gypsophilia buds amongst the foliage, then add a cluster of red alyssum in the centre and blue forget-me-nots here and there. Keep the design random with tiny florets softening the outline.

Now cut a white oval to fit the pendant. With the aid of toothpicks, fix two sprays of shepherd's purse foliage to the top and right of the card. Arrange flower stems to resemble the stems of a bunch of flowers. Now add curving gypsophilia buds throughout the design.

Add buds of spiraea and shepherd's purse next, teasing them into place, over dots of adhesive, with a soft paintbrush. Use an open flower of red alyssum to form the focal point and bring some spiraea through the design from the left to the centre. Assemble the jewellery according to the manufacturer's instructions.

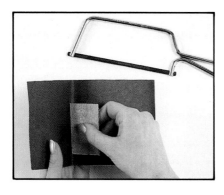

Make this delightful brooch from scratch! With a hacksaw cut a rectangle of thin mahogany 50mm by 75mm (2in by 3in). Round off the corners, front and back, with sandpaper. Give the brooch one thin coat of varnish and when completely dry, sand and varnish it again.

Form an outline on the sticky varnish with leaves of rock geranium, meadowsweet and common bent grass. Across this outline create a curving line of hawthorn flowers, tucking a few more leaves of rock geranium beneath the flowers as you go.

When the design is complete, coat with two or three layers of varnish, allowing each coat to dry in between applications. Finally, attach a brooch pin to the back of the wood with 'super' strong adhesive.

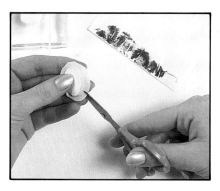

M any Victorian lockets or brooches were designed to take mementoes. This type of brooch is ideal for a miniature display of flowers. Cut a backing card to fit the brooch and cover it with foam. Now cut a larger oval from ivory silk and cover the foam with this. Make little snips into the overlapping edges of the silk as shown, wrap the edges round the backing card and glue down.

With latex adhesive fix a tip of frosted cow parsley leaf in the centre of the oval. At the top add pale peach candytuft and a wisp of common bent grass. Place more grass down the side of the design.

Add peach bistort to the left and red flowers of the spiraea 'Anthony Waterer' to the right and foreground. Finally, place an open flower of candytuft in the centre to form the focal point. Seal the design into the brooch using either the original backing or, if this is missing, packing it into an oval of thick cardboard.

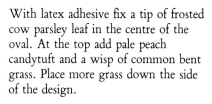

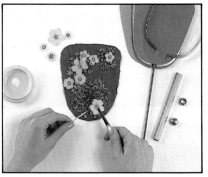

Plain dressing table sets such as this can be bought at good craft shops and from mail order craft suppliers. Dismantle the mirror and cut some cardboard to fit. Now cut a slightly smaller piece of foam to cover the cardboard. Cover both of these with some moss green silk. Fix on to the silk three heads of wild carrot, of various sizes, to form a soft, curving outline.

Using white potentilla (which turns a soft creamy colour when pressed) follow the outline, keeping the smaller flowers at the top and bringing the largest flower to the bottom centre. Complete with a head of wild carrot to create a strong focal point.

Repeat a similar design on the brush using two heads of wild carrot and slightly fewer potentillas. Assemble both brush and mirror according to the manufacturer's instructions.

─── SCIENTIFIC CLASSIFICATION ───

The following is an alphabetical list of the common names of plants
used in this book and their Latin equivalents.

Common name	Latin name	Common name	Latin name
Alyssum	*Alyssum*	Knotgrass	*Polygonum aviculare*
Apple blossom	*Malus sylvestris*	Lady's bedstraw	*Galium verum*
Astrantia	*Astrantia*	Lady's mantle	*Alchemilla alpina*
Ash	*Fraxinus excelsior*	Larkspur	*Delphinium consolida*
'Bachelor's Buttons'	*Ranunculus aconitifolius*	Lobelia	*Lobelia erinus*
buttercup		Loose silky bent grass	*Apera spica-venti*
Bamboo	*Arundinaria*	Love-in-a-mist	*Nigella damascena*
Bartonia	*Mentzelia lindleyi*	Maidenhair fern	*Adiantum pedatum*
Bearded twitch grass	*Agropyrom caninum*	Maple	*Acer campestre*
Beech	*Fagus sylvatica*	Meadow fescue	*Festuca pratensis*
Bistort	*Polygonum bistorta*	Meadowsweet	*Filipendula ulmaria*
Blackthorn	*Prunus spinosa*	Medick, yellow	*Medicago falcata*
'Blue Haze'	*Acaena*	Melilot	*Melilotus altissima*
Borage	*Borago officinalis*	Mind-your-own-business	*Helxine soleirolii*
Bottle sedge	*Carex rostrata*	Montbretia	*Crocosmia crocosmiiflora*
Bracken	*Pteridium aquilinum*	Mugwort	*Artemisia vulgaris*
Brome grass	*Bromus commutatus*	Norway maple	*Acer platanoides*
Buttercup	*Ranunculus acris*	Pansy	*Viola*
Camomile	*Matricaria matricariodes*	Pendulous sedge	*Carex pendula*
Candytuft	*Iberis umbellata*	Peony	*Paeonia lactiflora*
Carnation	*Dianthus carophyllus*	Periwinkle	*Vinca minor*
Carrot foliage (vegetable)	*Daucus carota*	Plumbago	*Plumbago capensis*
Cherry blossom	*Prunus sargentii*	Polyanthus	*Primula variablis*
Chervil	*Chaerophyllum temulentum*	Potentilla (shrubby)	*Potentilla furticosa*
Cocksfoot grass	*Dactylis glomerata*	Potentilla (woody)	*Potentilla nepalensis*
Common bent grass	*Agrostis tenuis*	Primrose	*Primula vulgaris*
'Copper Carpet'	*Acaena*	Quaking grass	*Briza media*
Cornflower	*Centaurea cyanus*	Reed canary grass	*Phalaris arundinacea*
Cow parsley	*Anthriscus sylvestris*	Rice grass	*Spartina townsendii*
Cow parsnip	*Heracleum sphondylium*	Rock geranium	*Geranium cinereum*
Cowslip	*Primula veris*	Rock rose	*Cistus*
Creeping bent grass	*Agrostis stolonifera*	Rose	*Rosa*
Creeping cinquefoil	*Potentilla reptans*	Rose bay willow herb	*Epilobium angustifolium*
Crested dog's tail grass	*Cynosurus cristatus*	Rough meadow grass	*Poa trivialis*
Daisy	*Bellis perennis*	Rue	*Ruta graveolens*
Delphinium	*Delphinium elatum*	Russian vine	*Polygonum aubertii*
Dogwood	*Cornus alba spaethii*	Rye grass	*Lolium perenne*
Elderflower	*Sabucus nigra*	Salad burnet	*Sanguisorba minor*
Euonymus	*Euonymus japonicus*	Saxifrage	*Saxifraxa moschata*
Fennel	*Foeniculum vulgare*	Shepherd's purse	*Capella bursa-pastoris*
Fern	*Polypodium*	Silverweed	*Potentilla anserina*
Feverfew	*Matricaria eximia*	Smokebush	*Cotinus coggygria*
Flowering currant	*Ribes sanguineum*	Snowdrop	*Galanthus nivalis*
Fools' parsley	*Aethusa cynapium*	'Sol d'Or'	*Narcissus jonquilla*
Forget-me-not	*Myosotis*	Southernwood	*Artemisia abrotanum*
Fuchsia	*Fuchsia magellanica*	Speedwell	*Veronica officinalis*
Geranium	*Pelargonium*	Spiraea (spring flowering)	*Spiraea arguta*
Geum	*Geum chiloense*	Spiraea (summer flowering)	*Spiraea bumalda*
Golden rod	*Solidago virgaurea*	Squirrel tailed fescue	*Vulpia bromides*
Greyhair grass	*Corynephorus canescens*	Star of Bethlehem	*Ornithogalum umbellatum*
Guelder rose	*Viburnum opulus*	Sumach	*Rhus typhina*
Gypsophilia	*Gypsophilia*	Sun rose	*Helianthemum nummularium*
Hairy tare vetch	*Vicia hirsuta*	Sweet cicely	*Myrrhis odorata*
Hare's tail grass	*Lagurus ovatus*	Thyme	*Thymus serpyllum*
Hawthorn	*Crataegus monogyna*	Traveller's joy	*Clematis vitalba*
Hazel	*Corylus avellana*	Tufted hair grass	*Deschampsia cespitosa*
Heart's ease	*Viola tricolor*	Verbena	*Verbena hybrida*
Heather	*Erica*	Vetch	*Vicia sativa*
Hebe	*Hebe*	Virginia creeper	*Parthenocissus quinquefolia*
Hedge bedstraw	*Galium album*	Water dropwort	*Oenanthe fistulosa*
Hedge parsley	*Torilis japonica*	Wayfaring tree	*Viburnum lantana*
Hop trefoil	*Trifolium campestre*	Whitebeam	*Sorbus aria*
Horseshoe vetch	*Hippocrepis comosa*	Wild carrot	*Daucus carota*
Hydrangea	*Hydrangea*	Wild strawberry	*Fragaria vesca*
Japanese crab apple	*Malus floribunda*	Willow	*Salix*
Japanese maple	*Acer palmatum*	Wood avens	*Geum urbanum*
Knapweed	*Centaurea nigra*	Yarrow	*Achillea millefolium*

ACKNOWLEDGEMENTS

The publishers would like to thank the following for their
help in compiling this book:

Longmans Ltd. Florist, 46 Holborn Viaduct, London EC1,
(for making the wedding bouquet on page 66).

Framecraft Miniatures Ltd., 148-150 High Street, Aston, Birmingham.

SUPPLIERS

Swan House Gallery, Ashfield, Stowmarket, Suffolk, England.
(Shop and mail order service run by author Mary Lawrence, specialized in the sale of pressed
flower accessories and designs, including presses, mounts, frames and wooden kits plus a
wide range of other items for displaying craftwork).

Mail order suppliers of items designed to display craftwork (such as porcelain
and crystal boxes, plaques, paperweights, fingerplates, napkin rings and vanity sets):

Framecraft Miniatures Ltd., 148-150 High Street, Aston, Birmingham, UK.
(supplying UK and Europe)

Anne Brinkley Designs, 21 Ransom Road, Newton Centre, Mass. 02159, USA.

Needlecraft International Pty. Ltd., 19 Railway Parade, Eastwood, NSW 2122, Australia.

Mrs Greville Parker, 286 Queen Street, Masterton, New Zealand.